# Moving to Tenerife: All You Need to Know

JOE CAWLEY

&

NICOLA QUINN

Please note that the advice given in the book is solely intended to serve as a guide and does not constitute legal advice. The publishers strongly advise anybody considering a move to Tenerife to seek specific help from relevant professionals.

# CONTENTS

# ACKNOWLEDGMENTS

Thanks to all those who provided information and helped in compiling facts and figures. Big thanks also to Janet Anscombe, one of Tenerife's experts-in-residence and a veritable fountain of local knowledge. See www.janetanscombe.com

# 1 INTRO

Hands up if you've ever been to Tenerife on holiday and toyed with the idea of making your stay a more permanent one.

No surprise, really – grey skies versus blue, roads clogged with stressed commuters versus a walk to work in the sunshine, wet weekends indoors versus days on the beach or round the pool.

In fact it's quite a wonder why more people don't bite the bullet and head for sunnier climes.

However, relocating can seem daunting – especially if you don't know much about the place. Hopefully with the help of this book, deciding if Tenerife is right for you, actually taking the plunge, and doing all the stuff that follows a move, should become a lot clearer.

*Moving to Tenerife is* a useful guide that will show you

the easiest path so you can begin enjoying your brand new life in the sun as soon as possible.

There are loads of different reasons why people decide to relocate to Tenerife and you need to make sure you want to move for all the right reasons – not the wrong ones. To clear things up, here's a list of the right and wrong reasons to move to Tenerife:

## The right reasons to move to Tenerife

### The climate

Although it may sound cliché, Tenerife really does enjoy sun all-year-round. The warm temperatures and pleasant sunshine can provide a world of relief for various aches and pains, including arthritis and sciatica, making it one of the favourite places to retire in. However, even if you're not at the end of your working life, always waking up to blue skies and sunshine has a remarkable effect on your mood throughout the day.

### Less stress

To us, the UK has become such a nanny state, putting all kinds of pressure on its inhabitants, with more 'Don't Do This' and 'Don't Do That' rules and regulations popping up than ever before. Sure there are rules to follow in Tenerife, but at least they also allow for a certain amount of common sense... which most of us are perfectly well equipped to use.

You'll also find that the 'keep up with your neighbours' attitude is not very prevalent in Tenerife. Most people couldn't give two monkeys what car you drive or whether you've got the fanciest washing machine in town. Far more important is how much you enjoy life when you're not working.

## Low cost of living

If you stick to local Spanish supermarkets, you'll find your cost of living to be much cheaper in Tenerife than in the UK. Take into consideration tiny petrol costs, a one-climate wardrobe, no heating bills and low rent and you're laughing. On the other hand, if you can't live without UK brands you'll find that although they're easily available, your weekly shopping bill isn't going to be as purse-friendly as it could be.

## Things to do

Tenerife may not be packed with state-of-the-art 3D cinemas and exciting theme parks like you'll find in the UK (the incredible Siam Park excepted), but the fantastic climate means that the island has built up a spectacular range of outdoor activities that you can enjoy throughout the year. With everything from windsurfing, sailing and golf to water parks, horse riding and camping available almost every day, you'll never be stuck for something to do. Weekends for the average Tenerife expat revolve around the pool, beach or mountain barbecues... all of which are free!

## Close to the UK

Depending on the relationship you have with your family, living 2,000 miles from friends and family can be a blessing or a curse. However, with flying time around four hours and over 200 connecting flights each week, it's easy to get from A to B without paying a fortune. At the time of writing, Ryanair, EasyJet and a number of other low-cost airlines operate an ever-expanding service from the UK so those trips back to visit Great Aunt Bethel can be as frequent as you like.

## The culture

The small Canarian villages seem tranquil and sleepy at a first glance, but just wait until it's fiesta time. Throughout the year, huge parties are thrown with giant paellas, displays of local handicrafts and lively Canarian music when people turn out in their best gear to celebrate. The Canarians are really welcoming people and will make you feel part of everything that's going on.

## You love Tenerife

Most people we know that have relocated to Tenerife holidayed several times a year on the island for years. Every time they looked out of the window on the plane at Tenerife South Airport they felt like their heart was breaking because they were leaving such a wonderful place. If this is how you feel, why not spare yourself the heartache and relocate?

## The wrong reasons to move to Tenerife

### You can't get work in the UK

If you're struggling to find work at home and think you'll be able to snap up a job in Tenerife – think again. Almost the whole world is struggling through rough times right now and decent jobs are hard to come by in Tenerife, just like anywhere else. At the time of writing, unemployment in the Canary Islands stands at around 33% (55% for the under 25s!)

On the other hand, there are a lot of unexplored niches in Tenerife, so if you have some creative ideas and want to work for yourself, this could be the land of opportunity!

### Alcohol and cigarettes are cheaper than the UK

It's true that nights out in Tenerife are much cheaper than in the UK – a pint of beer can be as cheap as €1 and cigarettes can be bought for as little as €6 for 200 – but is that *really* a good enough reason to up sticks and move?

### To run a bar

This is the most common misconception about moving

to Tenerife. When you're on holiday, you might get chatting to a British bar owner then suddenly start envisaging yourself living in Tenerife and running your own bar. After all, how hard can it be? It's more complicated and difficult than you can even imagine. Flip to the chapter on 'Supporting Yourself' to read more about running a bar in Tenerife or read about Joe's hilarious exploits when he attempted it, in his bestseller *More Ketchup than Salsa: Confessions of a Tenerife Barman* (available through Amazon).

## You're just fed up with the UK and want to live somewhere else

Living in the UK can get depressing at times, but why is moving to Tenerife going to improve your life? Are all of your problems centred around the UK, or would you just be bringing them with you if you moved to Tenerife? A change of scenery and a sun-filled day can greatly help, but it isn't going to solve *all* your problems just like that.

### It's Your Choice

Only *you* can decide if Tenerife really is the right place to begin your life – just make sure you're doing it for the right reasons and not the wrong ones.

A huge number of people relocate to Tenerife from the UK every year, but only a small percentage of them stay and make a success of it. Just remember that living in Tenerife isn't like being on holiday 24/7. You're not going to be able to lounge around in the sun every day and enjoy a few glasses of sangria at your local every evening – unless you're retiring, of course.

You and whoever you're moving with have to be 100% committed and up for it in order for you to even have a chance of succeeding. After you've gone through the hassle of finding a job, finding somewhere to live and sorting out all your documentation, Tenerife really is a fantastic place to live and will reward you with unforgettable memories for the rest of your life.

Nicola says:

"My parents made the initial decision to move to Tenerife but I chose to stay here after I left school and I'm confident I made the right choice for me. When I weighed up the pros and cons of living in the UK, I really struggled to come up with any positive points. I had no friends there, I wasn't familiar with any towns and the unemployment rate was rising, so my job prospects were bleak at best. What was there to go back for?

I intended to stay in Tenerife until I figured out exactly where I wanted to live – turns out it was Tenerife all along. I'm not saying I'll stay in Tenerife forever, but unless my next destination has fantastic weather, gorgeous beaches and a laid-back culture, I'm staying put."

Joe says:

"I originally moved to Tenerife to buy a bar/restaurant, with the full intention of making some money then moving back to the UK to start another business. When we sold the bar after an eight-year-slog of hard labour, we sent all our furniture back to the UK. Then, following several visits back to Blighty in search of another business, asked ourselves 'why are we moving back?'

Due to the absence of any good reason why we should swap life in Tenerife for the UK, we re-called all our possessions and have stayed here ever since. It's a combination of things that have kept us here, principally the weather, a more relaxed lifestyle and a healthier and safer environment to bring up my kids."

# 2 WHERE TO LIVE

Tenerife is a land of many landscapes *and* lifestyles and you need to choose which is going to suit you the most. Would you prefer a quiet rural life lolling in a frilly hammock in the hills and villages conversing with the goats and cacti, or mingling with friends in the resort areas, just a short stroll from all the beaches, bars and restaurants you could possibly dream of?

## NORTH OR SOUTH?

### Tenerife South

The vast majority of Tenerife arrivals turn left at the airport and head to the southern resorts with all its hotels, bars and restaurants. The same boxes that you tick when choosing your holiday accommodation are not the same as when you're searching for suitable long-term accommodation. For instance, most people would like a hotel close to the beach, nightlife and plenty of things to do. Perfect for a two-week getaway, but do you really want to be right in the thick of it 365 days a year?

Some holiday complexes offer apartments for long-term rent, but think twice before you dive in. If you rent an apartment in a holiday complex you'll be living amongst holidaymakers who aren't averse to staggering back to their apartment – possibly the one next door to yours – at 3 in the morning after a good night out.

There are a few residential complexes peppered amongst the hotels and apartments along the coast, but if you're looking for something bigger than a 2-3 bedroom apartment, you'll need to head further inland.

Generally, the further away from the coast you go, the cheaper and larger the accommodation – you can get a 4-bedroom villa with garden in a small Spanish village for about the same price as a 2-bedroom apartment in the centre of a tourist resort. It all comes down to what you'd rather have – a small place in the centre of it all or a lavish home a little further inland.

## Los Gigantes

One of the quieter resorts in the south, Los Gigantes is a favourite with retirees, despite its hills! There's not much going on here, with the exception of beautiful natural scenery and a central cluster of bars and restaurants. With facilities such as a bowling green and beautiful harbour you get the picture that this is not a town renowned for its fast pace of life.

You might also want to look at Puerto Santiago and Playa de la Arena nearby, both are home to a good mix of locals and expats and both offer a selection of tourist facilities side by side with authentic bars, cafes and shops.

**PROs:** peaceful atmosphere, picturesque surroundings, beautiful harbour, small friendly community

**CONs:** isolated from other main towns, limited nightlife, steep hills in Los Gigantes

### Playa de Las Americas

One of Tenerife's most popular holiday resorts sandwiched between Los Cristianos and Costa Adeje. The tacky nightclubs of the resort's heyday have been replaced with trendy cocktail bars, although party-loving visitors still thrive in their masses. If you want to be near the beaches, Brit bars and restaurants, this is the place for you. Having said that, there is also an enormous number of other nationalities that live here and add to the cosmopolitan feel - just don't expect to experience much of the 'real' Tenerife way of life.

**PROs:** central location, relatively flat, extensive public transport, great nightlife and choice of eateries

**CONs:** packed with holidaymakers, accommodation tends to be small, lots of noisy bars

## Los Cristianos

Whilst still commercialised, the quieter and more laid-back neighbour of Las Americas, Los Cristianos offers beautiful beaches and loads of quaint cafes frequented by locals. The area around Las Vistas beach is particularly popular with those of impaired mobility. The beach itself has superb facilities for the physically restricted and easy wheelchair access is common in lots of the nearby facilities.

**PROs:** central location, relatively flat, many shops, extensive public transport, great facilities for the mobility impaired

**CONs:** hilly away from the coast, difficult to find parking, accommodation can be expensive

## Costa Adeje

The shiny new boy in town. Although the dividing line between Las Americas and Costa Adeje is a little blurred, it's generally considered to be the area from Fañabe to La Caleta, plus the more remote Callao Salvaje and Playa Paraiso. This is where you'll find the newer and posher hotels – and also the higher prices. Upmarket properties abound behind the Playa del Duque but reasonably priced long-term accommodation can be found away from the beaches, particularly in places like Torviscas Alto and San Eugenio Alto.

**PROs:** more upmarket than Las Americas, less noisy bars and clubs, nice beaches, plenty of residential complexes

**CONs:** accommodation can be expensive near the coast, steep hills inland

### Golf del Sur

One of the smallest and quietest resorts on the island, Golf del Sur is popular with retirees and – you guessed it – golfers. Most of the action is centred around the San Blas square, with its various shops, cafes, bars and restaurants. It can seem a little isolated but many residents enjoy the 'village' feel, similar to the vibe found in the neighbouring 'sister' resort of Amarilla Golf.

**PROs:** everything you need in one resort, beautiful walking routes, golf courses

**CONs:** small resort, bars, restaurant and supermarkets are more expensive, can feel a bit isolated, under the airport flight path

### El Médano

Known as the bohemian resort, El Médano is the place to be if you enjoy water sports, a cosmopolitan vibe and a relaxed lifestyle. Although predominantly Canarian, there are a lot of different nationalities living in this seaside town.

**PROs:** friendly Canarian community, loads of water sports, beachfront location, young and sporty feel, relatively cheap accommodation

**CONs:** far from main resorts, often windy, small number of British residents, under the airport flight path

## Tenerife North

The north of the island is a completely different world to the south. The main variant you'll notice is the climate – the north can be cooler and damper than the sun-kissed south.

This isn't necessarily a deal-breaker when it comes to settling down – the cooler weather makes the north of the island greener and generally more picturesque than the dry, volcanic south so if you like skipping through flower-freckled meadows and suchlike... settle up north and go for it!

To be able to integrate up here however, you really need to speak Spanish (except in Puerto de la Cruz) because the further north and inland you go, the fewer people you'll come across with any grasp of English.

As in the south, the property prices are much higher in the centre of the resorts than the surrounding areas, so it's worth searching the outskirts for properties before jumping head first into the centre. The cheap cost of transport and fuel when compared to high rent and property prices will definitely see you better off.

## Santa Cruz

Tenerife's capital city – small enough to manage easily, whist being large enough to explore. As with most cities, Santa Cruz has a mixture of the good, the bad and the downright ugly. The old quarter at the bottom of Calle Nuria is gorgeous but the oil refinery end and residential area near the industrial centres are never going to win any beauty pageants. In fact they wouldn't be allowed to enter. However, with a smattering of parks and green areas, plus beautiful fishing villages further north like San Andrés, there are plenty of nice places you could call home. Speaking fluent Spanish is a must to get by and land a job here though, as the city is populated by almost 100% Spanish-speaking residents or African immigrants.

**PROs:** cosmopolitan feel, extensive public transport, many shops and cultural attractions

**CON:** traffic noise and pollution, some damn ugly buildings, expensive accommodation

## La Laguna

The island's university city, La Laguna offers a wealth of stunning architecture and a quiet way of life. Strong language skills are also needed here as you'll find very few nationalities other than Spanish-speakers.

**PROs:** beautiful architecture, cultural activities, many shops, good university

**CONs:** lack of English-speakers, difficult to park, cooler and damper weather, some seedy areas

## Puerto de la Cruz

Tenerife's first tourist resort was once a sleepy fishing village and still remains a little behind the times, in a good way. Speaking Spanish isn't as important here, as many people speak a little English though naturally you'll get more out of living in Puerto de la Cruz if you do make an effort to learn at least a bit of the lingo.

**PROs:** quiet atmosphere, beautiful surroundings, various attractions

**CONs:** old-fashioned, small resort, can be overcast

## RENT OR BUY?

### Renting a Property

The main advantage of renting a property (apart from the obvious cost) is the ability to move on easily if you decide the area – or even the island – isn't for you. You'll find properties for rent advertised in all the usual places – newspapers, estate agent windows and in the windows of the properties themselves. Additionally, try asking around in some of the local bars. As with anything in Tenerife, a lot of insider knowledge is gained by word of mouth.

Another huge advantage of renting is that there is minimal paperwork involved. Most landlords only require a *Residencia* and proof of ID, although you may be asked for your last three payslips if you're staying somewhere with a high rent. Most homes are rented fully-furnished so they're ready for you to move straight in.

There are two types of contracts – *contrato de arrendamiento de vivienda*/long-term contact which is valid for a minimum of one year, or the more common *contrato de arrendamiento por temporada*/short-term contact which is valid for three or six months. The long-term contact provides the tenant with a lot more legal protection than the short-term, which is why landlords are usually reluctant to hand them out. The short-term contracts are fully legal and can be changed into a long-term contract by the courts if you can prove it is your habitual home.

To be fully legal, contracts must be in Spanish, signed by landlord and tenant, and include ID numbers of both parties.

Most landlords will require a deposit (usually around the price of one month's rent) and the first month's rent paid up-front. Make sure you find out if you're paying a refundable deposit – you don't want any nasty surprises when it's time to leave. Some rentals include a certain amount for utilities – often up to €50 with the tenant being asked to pay for any extra when the bill arrives. Don't assume your rent covers this – ask the landlord and find out.

In addition to the contract, you should also get an inventory of the items in the property and the condition they are in. Make sure you check that everything is correct because if there is any discrepancy when your contract ends, you'll be the one forking out for missing or broken items.

As an example of rents, Joe pays around €700 per month plus bills for a three-bed farmhouse in a hillside village near Guia de Isora. Nicola pays around €600 plus bills for a two-bed duplex apartment on the seafront in La Tejita.

Buying Your Own Home

If you're absolutely, 100%, set-in-stone confident that Tenerife is going to be your long-term home, buying a property works out much more cost-effective than renting in the long-run. You'll find the same properties listed in various newspapers and estate agent windows for different prices, so it's worth having a look around to find the cheapest before making a bid.

There are loads of English-speaking estate agents on the island but two that we recommend are the Tenerife Property Shop S.L. (www.tenerifepropertyshop.com;

+34 922 714 700) and Tenerife Property Sales (www.tenerifepropertysales.com; +34 922 861 313).

If you're not confident with your level of Spanish, consider asking a trustworthy Spanish-speaking friend to accompany you throughout the process to make sure you understand what's going on. If nobody comes to mind, you could always pay for an interpreter – yes, it will cost you, but understanding what you're signing could cost you a lot less in the long-run.

If your offer is accepted by the estate agent, you'll have to fork out a deposit of around 10% before anything commences. After paying the deposit, it's wise to get a lawyer involved as soon as you can. There are mountains of paperwork involved in purchasing a property in Tenerife and your dream could quickly become a nightmare if you get landed with a large fine for filling out paperwork incorrectly or get pressured into signing something you don't understand.

After paying the deposit, the estate agent will apply for a *Nota Simple* from the Land Registry which will reveal if there are any outstanding charges on the property. In Tenerife any unpaid charges on the property become yours when you buy it, so it is crucial you understand everything you sign.

The estate agent will then draw up a *Compraventa* which is a purchase and sale agreement that you and the sellers will need to sign.

Crossing the Ts and dotting the Is should take around 4-6 weeks, after which you'll have to take a trip to the Notary to finalise the paperwork.

Be prepared for long delays, mix-ups and multiple disasters during the procedures. Anything with paperwork involved seems to take a lifetime in Tenerife – keep reminding yourself that it will be worth it in the end.

In addition to the price of the property, here is a list of taxes, fees and all the other little extras that you'll have to pay when buying a property in Tenerife.

Tax: Either 6.5% ITP (*Impuesto sobre Transmisiones Patrimoniales*, a transfer tax) for resale properties or 7% IGIC (*Impuesto General Indirecto de Canarias*, equivalent to VAT) for new properties. New properties also require stamp duty 0.75% AJD (*Impuesto sobre Actos Jurídicos Documentados*, a document registration tax).

Notary fee: This varies depending on the value of the property. The minimum is €300, but you should expect to pay between €500 and €1,000.

Land registry: Registering your property in the municipal land registry will cost around half of the Notary fee.

*Plusvalía*: This is based on the size of the property and can range anywhere from a few hundred Euros to a few thousand. This is a tax on the increase in assessed value of the land on which a property is located during the seller's ownership. The seller is legally obliged to pay this, but more often than not, the buyer ends up copping it when the seller has left the island.

## Buying to Let

If you're planning on buying a property in Tenerife with the intentions of letting it out, be very careful – if you end up breaking one of the rules you'll be in a lot of trouble and recently the authorities have been clamping down hard on anybody letting on a residential complex without the correct papers, and/or using anybody other than the sole, authorised management or letting agency for your complex. The letting law is a minefield, so don't believe an estate agent if they say words to the effect of "oh, it's alright, everybody rents their apartment out these days." Not anymore they don't!

### Short-term lets

The rules on letting out tourist apartments and holiday homes are different depending on the municipality in which the property is located. It's best to check with your local town hall to find out exactly which rules apply to you.

The general trend seems to be that if you want to rent out a property for short term on a tourist complex, you'll be fined unless you use the registered managing agent on site. If your complex doesn't have an agent/management company, or less than 51% of the owners agree to rent out their property, you're stuck and can't legally rent out to holidaymakers. You'd think it would simply be a case of trekking to the town hall and applying for a licence to rent your property out but no, at the time of writing the government is no longer issuing touristic licences.

**Long-term lets**

Long-term letting is a lot simpler and doesn't require you to apply for a special licence. Just be sure to double check that you're using the correct contract – *arriendos de vivienda* are for between one and five years and *arriendos de temporada* are for one year or less.

Whether you rent or buy, it's highly likely that you're going to need more than a couple of Tesco bags to shift your gear across the water. Contact Universal Exports (www.removals-tenerife.com; (00 44) 07973 222389) and let them sort out the removal logistics for you.

Dealing with Utility Companies

Oh utility companies... how we love thee. Not.

As any Tenerife resident will tell you, one of the most undeniably frustrating aspects of living in the Canary Islands is having to deal with utility companies whose customer service departments are staffed with nothing but poorly trained and misguided souls whose only intention is to either confound the heck out of you or provide as much help as a paper fire hose. You have been warned!

Thankfully, when renting a property, the utilities will be taken care of by the landlord. To avoid nasty shocks, make sure you check whether your rent covers all, part or none of the utility bills.

If you plan on buying a property, you'll have to deal with all the utility companies yourself (lucky you) although it might pay to use a Spanish-speaking admin helper. Endesa (www.endesaonline.com) is the company in charge of electric and Entemanser (www.entemanser.com) is in charge of water. Although both of these companies have websites, you'll have to phone or walk into an office if you need to sort out any problems.

Remember, electricity is 220 volts in Tenerife (240v in the UK), but all your home appliances should work fine, you'll just need a two-pin adapter plug for the Tenerife sockets.

Movistar (www.movistar.es) is the company in charge of all the phone lines and consequently internet connection. This is the company that most expats hate getting involved with the most. Because Movistar has the Canaries monopolised, the company doesn't have to worry about the little things like training staff or providing even a modicum of courtesy when dealing with customers.

You can pop into any of the Movistar shops when signing up for a service, but if you have any problems or want to terminate a contract, you'll have to call the company. Ironically, you're almost guaranteed to get dreadful line quality and even if you speak perfect Spanish, you'll have a hard time getting your point across. You can request to speak to someone in English; dial 1004 and just say 'Inglés' (een-glaze) whenever there's a gap in the automated responder. Sometimes it works, sometimes it doesn't... a bit like everything in Tenerife.

Nicola says:

"Since moving to Tenerife, I've lived in a variety of homes and locations – a large townhouse on an industrial estate, a small apartment on a tourist resort and now a duplex by the beach in a very quiet village. I love being able to walk along the deserted beach on an evening, but miss the convenience of having shops, restaurants and other people nearby. The complex we live in is mainly used by Canarians as their summer houses, so during August and some weekends, the place is packed, but for the rest of the year we practically have it all to ourselves.

This is great when we want some peace and quiet, but at other times it can be a bit lonely. The buses stop at about 10pm, so if we fancy a night out away from the local *chiringuito*, we have to fork out about €30 for a taxi."

Joe says:

"I've lived on both sides of the fence – on a predominantly tourist-orientated seafront complex and now in a quiet village in the hills. Although we have a view of the sea, I do miss being just a walk from the coast but this is outweighed by the sheer peacefulness of life in the hills. In the evening, all I can hear is birdsong and the occasional dog barking across the valley. I'm also just a short distance from plenty of nature walks, and can reach the nearest beach in less than 15 minutes by car. Our house is at a height of 670 metres, which means that we also feel the change of seasons more profoundly than those living on the coast. In winter we light a log fire, with morning temps of around 10-11 degrees C. However, as it doesn't get quite as hot in summer, sleep comes a lot easier to us hill-folk during July and August! Finally, living in a Canarian village means we don't pay the prices that resort-dwellers pay. For instance, a cup of coffee or a bottle of beer is just €1 in the local bar and the local corner shop stocks everything we need at around 20% less cost than resort supermarkets. Although I'm sure it's not for everybody, I'm more than happy to live up here in the 'real Tenerife'."

JOE CAWLEY & NICOLA QUINN

# 3 EDUCATION

One of the top things on every parent's list when relocating is getting their child into a decent school. Child-free readers can happily skip by this chapter, but it may be worth scanning through for future use or just to help out a friend.

The first decision you need to make is whether you want your ankle-biters following the British or Spanish system. You've got to be pretty sure of your decision because although it's possible to do so, it's unadvisable to change systems during schooling because both follow separate curriculums.

## The British System

<u>PROS</u>

**Classes are in English:** The children are taught all their lessons in English, so nothing will be lost in translation. Spanish lessons are given daily and, although it is unlikely they will become fluent in the language without any additional classes or practice, they will be able to speak it at a high level.

**Same curriculum:** British schools in Tenerife follow the UK curriculum, so if you're relocating half way through the school year, your child will be able to pick up right from where they left off without any hassle.

**Freedom to choose:** If you decide to send your child to a British school, you can visit the schools and chat with the teachers to find the one which suits your child best.

<u>CONS</u>

**High cost:** Sending a child to a British school comes with an ever-increasing price tag because they're all private. Although you won't usually have to pay for any text books, you will have to fork out a large sum for the uniform, transport and food as well as the school fees.

**Wasted qualifications:** If your child wants to continue living in Tenerife or any other Spanish country after they've left school, their qualifications will be almost completely redundant. Only the British companies on the island recognise IGCSEs – the qualifications achieved through the British system – whereas they will be meaningless to Spanish companies.

**Lack of friends:** The children who attend British schools travel from all over the island and it's quite likely that you won't be living close to your child's friends. If they only have friends from school, you'll end up spending most of your evenings and weekends driving back and forth to their friends' houses.

Here's a list of all the British schools in Tenerife:

Wingate (www.wingateschool.com) in Cabo Blanco is open to pupils aged three to 18.

The British School (www.britishschooltenerife.com) in Puerto de la Cruz teaches children from age one to 18.

St Andrew's School in El Sauzal (www.saintandrewstenerife.com) accepts students aged three to 12.

Callao Learning Centre in Callao Salvaje (www.callaolearning.org) is different to the other private British schools on the island. It is a preparation school for mainstream education and accepts a variety of ages. This school also supports flexible attendance – pupils can attend daily, weekly or monthly.

The Spanish System

The Spanish school days are significantly shorter than

those of the British system. Primary schools usually begin around 9am and finish at 2pm (1pm in June and September). School days at secondary schools are a bit longer, with days usually beginning at 8.30am and ending at 2.20pm. Since it's difficult for a lot of parents to collect their children at these times, free or low-cost bus services are usually provided by the school.

The school year is divided into three terms, much like the British system. Two to three weeks for Christmas – usually the Friday before Christmas until the first weekday after January 7th, one week for Easter and ten to 11 weeks for summer – from the last week of June until the first week of September. There are no half-term holidays, but this is more than made up for by the abundance of fiesta days throughout the year.

<u>PROS</u>

**They'll pick up the language fast:** All lessons are taught in Spanish, so children grasp the language much faster than they would at a British school. Most Spanish schools supply an English-speaking assistant to help your child get to grips with it faster. This isn't just an advantage for the child – you'll be surprised how much you'll pick it up, too.

**It's (almost) free:** Spanish schools do not charge a penny for your child to attend, but there are a few hidden costs. You'll be provided with a list at the beginning of the school year with everything they'll need – including books and stationary – which you'll have to provide and pay for.

**Qualifications count:** If your child continues living in Tenerife – or any other Spanish country – the qualifications they gained at school will be widely recognised. The qualifications earned during *El Bachillerato* (the Spanish equivalent of sixth form) are also recognised when applying to most European universities.

<u>CONS</u>

**Lost in Translation:** Moving to a different country and leaving family and friends behind is stressful enough for a child without dropping them in the deep end when it comes to language. In Spanish schools, nearly all lessons are taught in Spanish, but no matter what age your child is, they will soon pick it up.

**Lack of choice:** You can't decide which school you want your child to attend – they must attend one of the schools in the same municipality in which you live.

**Paperwork:** You're probably beginning to see a recurring theme when it comes to living in Tenerife: masses of paperwork. If you want to get your child into a Spanish school, you're going to have to get yourself organised and sort out all your paperwork months before term starts.

You'll need the *Residencias* of both parents and the

child, your *Libro de Familia* if your child was born in Spain, or a birth certificate if they were born elsewhere, your latest *Declaración de la Renta* and medical documentation to support any disability or illness your child has. It's worth making photocopies of all the paperwork, too. You're almost always required to produce your own photocopies of documents, even if there's a photocopier in the building. You'll also need to fill out a form requesting a place for your child (you can find the form for pre-school and primary at www.gobiernodecanarias.org/educacion). You'll have to collect the form for secondary and sixth-form from the school and hand it in to the school you're applying for.

## It's Your Choice

When it comes down to it, whether you send your child to a private British school or a state-run Spanish school is entirely your call. You can ask around, but you're guaranteed to get widely varying opinions and contrasting stories which probably aren't going to help you out much.

Nicola says:

"I was educated in a private British school from age 11 until 16 and I achieved fantastic grades – although I think this was due to spending a lot of my spare time studying. Keep in mind that the private British schools in Tenerife are not necessarily on par with the ones in the UK – they are primarily a business, not always a place to nurture pupils and encourage growth. After leaving school I could speak Spanish well but I wasn't fluent and my qualifications meant absolutely nothing to all the Spanish companies that I applied to, which left me waiting tables two years. Looking back, I think attending a Spanish school would have been a better move for me because I'd be much more confident with the language, would fit more comfortably into the culture and would have many more career opportunities open to me in Spain. "

Joe says:

"My two kids have been attending local Spanish school from age three. They're now eight and ten and are both fully bi-lingual, switching from one language to another without a thought. Although they both struggled initially and didn't join in for months, they're like little sponges and were absorbing absolutely everything they heard. I found the level of infant and primary education fantastic and with class sizes varying between eight and 15 students, the teachers have time to give everyone plenty of personal attention. I can't vouch for secondary education (*instituto*), but so far, I'm glad my kids have been educated the local way at a Spanish school."

# 4 BECOMING LEGAL

Another minefield when it comes to Tenerife bureaucracy is becoming legal. Many people arrive on the island, lie low and stay out of the system. We wouldn't advise this. Partly because you could find yourself in all kinds of bother if found out and partly because you'll miss out on a lot of potential benefits.

But... there's no denying that getting all of your documentation in order can be one of the most confusing, frustrating and time-consuming things you'll have to do in Tenerife. Whatever you're applying for, take our advice... go armed with every little bit of paperwork you can lay your hands on - passport, driving licence, bank statement, rental contract, birth certificate, marriage certificate, doctor's note, lottery ticket, laundry receipt etc... and all with accompanying photocopies. Chances are there'll still be something missing that you weren't told about, but this is part of the Tenerife paper chase so don't get too stressed... we all have to go through it.

For more information on legalities for expats, you'll find the locally-revered local expert, Janet Anscombe (www.janetanscombe.com) a fountain of knowledge and glad to help!

These are the current procedures to obtain the most important documents in Tenerife:

## *Certificado de Empadronamiento* (Certificate of Citizenship)

A *Certificado de Empadronamiento* is a document which proves that you live in a municipality within Spain. You'll need this to register at a medical centre, to get married, to register yourself as a resident and to enjoy discounted travel for residents. Each *Certificado de Empadronamiento* is only valid for six months, so you'll have to go to the town hall to renew it if you need it more than six months after it was issued.

You'll need:

- Passport
- Copy of passport
- Proof of address (house deeds, rental contract, utility bill – anything with your name and address on will do)
- €1.80 (for tax)

Method One: In Person

1. Grab your documentation and head to your town hall.
2. Tell the receptionist that you want to register for the *Certificado de Empadronamiento*. They'll ask you for €1.80 tax and print it there and then.

Method Two: Online

This option is only available in certain municipalities: Arona, Guia de Isora, San Miguel de Abona, Granadilla de Abona, Guimar, Vilaflor, La Guancha, Santa Ursula, Santa Cruz, La Laguna and El Sauzal at the time of writing.

1. Log on to your municipality's town hall website.
2. Search for the *Certificado de Empadronamiento* application page in the search bar and follow the instructions there.

## *Certificado Registro Residente* (Certificate of a Registered Resident)

A *Certificado Registro Residente* is a document which proves you're a resident in Spain. This is the most important document and the one which you'll be asked to show the most. It's a small green credit-card sized piece of paper which displays your details including your NIE (Foreigners' National Identity) number which will be allocated when you register as a resident if you haven't already got one, as you're required to do by law when you've been in Spain for three months.

How long this process will take you all depends on when you go. Some days you could be waiting hours, whereas other days you could be in and out within minutes – it really is just the luck of the draw. The busiest time is usually between 8am and 9am on a Monday morning, so if you avoid going at that time, you should get the whole thing over with relatively quickly.

You'll need:

- Passport
- One photocopy of your passport
- One passport-sized photo
- Original and in-date *certificado de empadronamiento*
- One black pen
- €10.30 (for tax)

You'll also need:

**If you're working:** the original and a copy of your current work contract or certificate to show you're making social security payments

**If you're self-employed:** the original and a copy of your self-employment documentation and a certificate to show you're making social security payments

**If you're retired:** proof of income sufficient to support you and your family, plus the original and a copy of your private health insurance or a copy of your S1 document or a valid European health card.

1. Head to the nearest National Police station and pick up a *Certificado Registro Residente* request form and a 790 tax slip from the information desk. Fill out the form as much as you can. If you're stuck on a few words a quick online search will help you out.

2. Head to the nearest bank, hand over the 790 slip and pay the €10.30 tax.  The bank teller will stamp your form and hand it back to you.

3. Return to the police station and queue up for the information desk again. Show the member of staff your completed form and your stamped 790. You will be given a numbered ticket for a desk. Sit in the chairs and wait until your number is called.

4. When your number appears on the screen, go to the desk and hand your forms over, along with the rest of the documentation.

5. The police officer will print your *Certificado Registro Residente* there and then.

## *Número de Seguridad Social* (Social Security Number)

Social Security in Tenerife is similar to National Insurance in the UK. With this number you can get a legal work contract, receive unemployment benefits and sign up at a medical centre.

A new rule was introduced in 2012, making it only possible for people to obtain a social security number if they can prove they have a means to support themselves in either of the following ways;

One: If you've received a job offer and need a social security number for a work contract so you can pay into the system. If this is the case, you'll need to take proof of the job offer in the form of a Spanish letter.

Two: If you're retired and need a social security number to sign up at a medical centre. If this is the case you'll need to provide your S1 health entitlement documentation.

You'll need:

- Proof of job offer or S1 health entitlement documentation
- Passport
- Copy of passport
- *Certificado Registro Residente*
- Copy of *Certificado Registro Residente*
- Black pen
- Patience!
- Somebody who can speak Spanish... or a damn good Spanish/English dictionary

1. Gather your documentation and head to the nearest Social Security office.

2. Tell the person at the information desk that you want a *Número de Seguridad Social*.
3. Fill out the form they give you and return to the information desk.
4. You'll be handed a numbered ticket. Wait until it's your turn then go to the appropriate desk. Hand over your paperwork and in a few minutes you'll be presented with your social security number.

## *Certificado de Viajes* (Travel Certificate)

A *Certificado de Viajes* is a document which allows you to travel within Spain with a Canary Islands resident discount – currently 50%, so not to be sniffed at! It's very similar to the *Certificado de Empadronamiento*, in that it states that you're a resident of a municipality within Spain and is obtained in the same way. You don't need to get a hold of a certificate every time you travel – each one is valid for six months. The *Certificado de Viajes* isn't enough to travel on its own – you'll also need your passport.

Several companies have now begun using SARA (*Sistema Acreditación Residencia Automático*) which allows agents and airlines to confirm electronically that you're a resident in Spain without you having to do anything. There is no solid list of which airlines follow this practice, so it's best to be safe and get a hold of the document anyway.

You'll need:

- Passport
- Copy of passport
- *Certificado Registro Residente*
- Proof of address (house deeds, rental contract, utility bill – anything with your name and address on will do)

Method One: In Person

1. Grab your documentation and head to your town hall.
2. Tell the receptionist that you want to register for the *Certificado de Viajes*. After a few taps of the keyboard, they'll print it out there and then.

Method Two: Online

This option is only available in certain municipalities: Arona, Guia de Isora, San Miguel de Abona, Granadilla de Abona, Guimar, Vilaflor, La Guancha, Santa Ursula, Santa Cruz, La Laguna and El Sauzal at the time of writing.

1. Log on to your municipality's town hall website.
2. Search for the *Certificado de Viajes* application page in the search bar and follow the instructions there.

Nicola says:

"Don't let all the horror stories chew you up inside. Providing you speak a decent level of Spanish – or have a Spanish-speaker with you – and are armed with every government-issued piece of paper you own, you should be able to get the job done. One bit of advice: don't even bother leaving the house without photocopies of each document. The photocopier might only be an arm's length away from you at the police station, but there is no way they're going to let you use it."

Joe says:

"There's no denying the Canarian bureaucratic system is a nightmare, especially for anybody who doesn't speak the language. If you want to sleep easy at night, there's no choice... roll up your sleeves, gather every bit of paperwork you've ever collected in your life, employ the services of an interpreter and prepare to go to battle. Oh... and *buena suerte* (good luck)!"

JOE CAWLEY & NICOLA QUINN

# 5 SUPPORTING YOURSELF

Deciding that you want to pack up your troubles in an old kit bag and start your new life on a sunny holiday island is all well and good, but when you arrive what are you actually going to do? When you're on holiday, it's all too easy to imagine yourself lounging by the pool with a cocktail, but in reality, life in Tenerife is nothing like that. Just like anywhere else, there are bills to pay and things to buy. Where's the money going to come from?

## Your Options

Although Tenerife's economy is built on the tourism sector, this doesn't mean your career prospects are limited to bar work. Any experience with computers, accounting, secretarial work or real estate will certainly come in handy. There are several options available for manual work, too, such as mechanics, plumbing, electrics and carpentry.

If you scan through the adverts, most of the jobs you see will be for bar work, restaurant servers, PRs, telemarketers and timeshare salespeople. Although you may cringe at the thought of being stood on the street at night trying to get people into a bar, don't dismiss it. I've worked in bars, restaurants and done a bit of PR-ing and even though you won't be rolling in cash, it can help pay the bills.

These sort of jobs generally come with plenty of spare time during the day, so you can really enjoy the island, too. When I first began PR-ing for a restaurant, I would spend the day lounging on the beach, before strolling into work at around 7pm, chatting to a few happy tourists and would have finished for the night by about 11pm. I did come across a few people who really weren't interested in talking to me at all, but overall I had a fantastic time and it really didn't feel like work most of the time.

Entertainers are highly called for on the island, too, so if you have any experience performing – singing, dancing or a speciality act – have a chat with a few bars that offer entertainment or speak to other entertainers and see if they can give you a few tips on getting a slot. Bear in mind though that competition is increasing just as rates are decreasing. As in the UK, the recent recession has a firm grip on Tenerife too.

## Finding a Job

Languages are valued highly in Tenerife and the more you can speak, the greater your chance of getting a job. In addition to English, being able to speak Spanish is the first language employers will look for, followed by German, French and other European languages. At the time of writing, English/Russian speakers are also highly sought after, especially in the property market.

There's almost no point in applying for work unless you're on the island. There could be hundreds of people applying for the same position you're interested in and you'll be well down the list if you're not even on the island yet.

It's often the case of *it's not what you know, but who you know* in Tenerife, so networking with people is a great way to hear about vacancies and job offers. You'll find jobs advertised in newspapers, on the radio and online on the Oasis FM job page (www.oasisfm.com/jobs) and the Tenerife Forum job section at www.tenerifeforum.org.

## Work Contracts

If you get a job working in a bar or restaurant, it's often the case that you won't be offered a work contract and the minute the police show up to check paperwork, you'll be hidden in the back room – believe me, I've been there! Employers don't like handing out contracts because it costs them a lot of money – they have to pay a large chunk of your social security as well as your salary. Unfortunately, if you start making a fuss about contracts and working illegally, instead of getting a contract, you'll probably just get the sack and they'll employ the next person in line desperate for a job.

If you are fortunate enough to be offered a legal contract with your job, congratulations! You should first receive a *Contrato Temporal* (temporary contract) which is valid for three months. This contract will include a clause which states that the company can get rid of you in the first two months without severance pay if they decide you're not right for the job.

If your employer is happy with you after your first three months, you should get another *Contrato Temporal* valid for either three, six or nine months. After working for a company for 12 months, you're entitled to a *Contrato Indefinido* (indefinite contract). A *Contrato Indefinido* is considered to be the crème de la crème of work contracts because they're very hard to come by. Employers rarely hand these contracts out because if they decide to get rid of you for no good reason, they'll have to pay you a large sum in redundancy pay.

One of the clauses often buried in contracts states that an employee has already 'resigned' in advance. This type of clause is actually illegal, but what's the point in battling a legality war when you're sacked and being told you've already resigned voluntarily? Make sure you get a copy of your contact and go over it line by line so you understand exactly what you're being asked to sign.

Unemployment Benefits

If your contract is terminated, you should get a letter from your employer and a *Certificado de Empresa* which lists how much salary you have received whilst working for the company.

To receive unemployment benefit, you'll need to pop into your nearest unemployment office as soon as possible – you only have 15 days after being laid off to do this, otherwise your benefit will be reduced. You'll need to take your *Certificado de Empresa* and birth certificates of any children living in your home with you.

You'll be asked what kind of work you're looking for and if anything comes up, they'll set up an interview for you, just like they would in the UK. It's important to attend every interview they organise otherwise your benefit could be stopped.

Unemployment benefit isn't available for everyone. To claim you must have worked on the island for at least 360 days within the last six years. The amount you receive will depend on the amount of contributions you've made within the last 180 days. Be aware that you won't receive unemployment benefit forever – it will stop after a maximum of two years. After the benefit stops, you will be eligible to receive a monthly payment of around €400 for six months – providing you can prove that you've been actively seeking work. If you still haven't found a job after that, then you're on your own and any kind of funding stops.

## Working for Yourself

One of the reasons people decide to relocate is because they want to get away from a dull, repetitive lifestyle. One of the aspects of this monotony is a dead-end 9-5 job. What better way to start afresh than open up your own business and be your own boss? The idea may sound fantastic, but there are loads of things to consider before making the leap.

Firstly you need to decide on your target market – are you focusing on tourists or residents? Then you need to decide what product or service you're going to offer and whether it will be of any benefit to the people of Tenerife. Choosing a location is of great importance, too, and let's not forget how vital an internet presence can be.

A great way to research and find out more info is to look into other businesses which are similar to the one you're thinking of running. Study how they do business, how they advertise and what their reputation is.

## Tax for Self-Employed

If you're planning on becoming self-employed and opening your own business, it's up to you to make sure your taxes are paid. You should go to the Tax Office and tell them you want to sign up as *Autonomo* (self-employed). You'll have to fill out a document with your personal details and details about your business so they can work out how much tax you'll need to pay.

There are two tax systems in Tenerife: *Modelo* and *Estimación Directa*.

With the *Modelo* system, your tax is calculated based on what you do in your business, the size of the building and an estimation as to what your income is likely to be. Because of this, there is no need to keep a hold of any invoices, receipts or accounts if you don't want to and if your business is busier than expected, you could end up paying less tax than if you'd used the other method.

With the *Estimación Directa* system, you keep track of your accounts, receipts and invoices then your tax is calculated on your actual income and expenditure – much like the system in the UK.

If you opt for the *Modelo* system first, you can change to the *Estimación Directa* whenever you choose, but you can't do it the other way round.

The old rule was that unless your business took more than €28,000 in the first year of trading, you didn't have to pay IGIC (the Spanish equivalent of VAT). However, starting from January 1$^{st}$ 2013, there is no exemption for first year trading and you have to pay IGIC regardless of turnover. IGIC is much lower in Tenerife than VAT in the UK and the rate varies according to the type of business.

In addition to tax, you'll also have to pay social security. You'll start off by paying around €260 per month which will gradually increase each year.

There are advantages and disadvantages to being *autonomo*, so seek further advice from a reputable, English-speaking gestoria or accountant such as Marcos Cabrera in Los Cristianos (+34 922 794 313).

## Buying an Existing Business

It's easy to get confused when buying a business in Tenerife simply because of the language difference. *Trespaso* refers to the business itself and *Local/Locales* refers to the building/buildings. If you buy a business, you won't own the building, so you'll be required to pay a monthly rent to the owner.

Before jumping into anything, make sure you find out why the owner is selling the *Trespaso* – you don't want to find out that it's because no people ever walk by and the owner is making no money. Perhaps spend a day or two making a footfall count, making note of how many and what type of people walk past the business in a day. If the business is a shop or bar and is still open, stop by on different days at different times to see how busy it is. Don't be afraid to ask to see the accounts.

You'll find businesses for sale in estate agents' windows, newspapers and in the businesses themselves. We also recommend you take a look at Tenerife Business Sales (www.tenerifebusinesssales.com).

## Starting a New Business

If you plan on opening up a new business, it's best to get a *Gestor* (admin manager) involved from the word go. There's an unbelievable amount of paperwork involved and you'll be fined heavily if you fill out paperwork incorrectly or are missing documents during an inspection.

One of the most important documents every business needs to have is an opening licence. Opening licences are issued per activity – not per business – so if your business deals with more than one activity, you'll need several opening licences.

Make sure you tell your *Gestor* exactly what you're planning to do – don't leave anything out! Although he/she will be expensive, they really want to help you but won't be at fault if you get fined for them filling out a form incorrectly because you've held back information.

## Running Your Own Bar

It's all too easy to get swept up in the romantic idea of living on a holiday island and running your very own bar. Long, lazy days spent lounging on the beach, followed by exciting buzzing evenings chatting to friends in your bar. This may be how it pans out in your head, but it doesn't even come close to the reality of it. Just ask Joe, he ran a bar for eight years then wrote a book about it. *Read More Ketchup than Salsa: Confessions of a Tenerife Barman* (available on Amazon.co.uk and Amazon.com) for a hilarious insight into just some of the traumas and disasters he faced by choosing this popular expat career.

You'll find many bars for sale in estate agents' windows, but be warned – you must have your wits about you. Estate agents are very familiar with people jetting over from the UK and wanting to buy a bar. Just remember, they don't all have your best interests at heart – many just want your cash. If you can, try and get in touch with the landlord directly – estate agents add their own fees on top of their clients' asking prices, so you're guaranteed to get a better deal if you can cut out the middle man completely. If you do this though, always seek legal help and advice from a neutral lawyer i.e. not the lawyer recommended by the bar owner!

Paperwork is a very tricky business for bar owners and is much different to that of the UK. You'll need an opening licence for every activity which will take place in your bar – the selling of drinks, the selling of food, live entertainment, karaoke, TVs and even just to play the radio. Hefty fines come for anyone breaking the rules – even if you're innocently unaware of them – so it's wise to get a *Gestor* involved to make sure

(IPC) in the UK.

MOVING TO TENERIFE: ALL YOU NEED TO KNOW

everything is squeaky clean.

If you've ever owned or even worked in a bar before then you're miles ahead in experience than the rest of the crowd. Even if you're confident you can run a bar well, what about getting yourself established in the first place? You need to create an environment that people will want to be in, offer something that the surrounding bars don't (entertainment, cheaper prices...) and most importantly, you need to stand out above the crowd. You'll be surprised how much a lick of paint and a few comfy chairs can make when people are deciding where they want to go for a drink or snack.

Although it can be a wonderful experience and a fantastic success for some people, for the majority it ends in heartache. We can think of dozens of stories of people coming over to the island with wads of cash and happy smiles, only to leave six months later without a penny to their name – don't let the next one be you.

Retiring and Pensions

You can receive a UK pension in any EU country, so you shouldn't have a problem in Tenerife. You'll receive it the same way you did in the UK – being paid straight into your bank account or by post.

If you've paid National Insurance in the UK, about four months before you reach retirement age, you'll receive a claim form from the International Pensions Centre (IPC) in the UK.

If you're living in Tenerife when you retire and have paid social security here, you shouldn't use the UK form. You need to claim through the *Centros de Atención y Información de la Seguridad Social del Instituto Nacional de la Seguridad Social* in Tenerife, attaching the UK letter to the Spanish application form.

If you live in Tenerife but have never paid social security on the island, you can claim your pension directly from the IPC.

Nicola says:

"I've only ever been an employee and have therefore had almost all of my paperwork taken care of by the company I work for. The only piece of advice I can give you about work contracts is don't believe anything unless you've seen it. If your employer claims to be making social security payments on your behalf, ask to see the paperwork or if the company insists you've moved up from a *Temporal* contract to an *Indefinido*, make sure you get a copy."

Joe says:

"I've been an employee, and employer and now an *autonomo* (sole-trader). All involve different, and often convoluted, processes regarding paperwork and all have their advantages and pitfalls. Even if you're an employee, there are still certain administrative obligations required so seek help from an expert."

# 6 HEALTH CARE

Just because you're relocating doesn't mean you have to compromise when it comes to health care. Many people consider the Spanish health service – both the private sector and the state-run service – to be better than that in the UK and one of the best in Europe.

Private Health Care

There are several companies that offer private health care in Tenerife. Two of the most popular are Adeslas and DKV, both valid in various hospitals in the north and south of the island. Most doctors and specialists speak a high level of English and if yours doesn't, the hospital will supply an interpreter for free.

If you're covered by private health insurance and need medical care, you'll need to visit your nearest private consultant. After an examination, the doctor will either give you a prescription there and then or will write you a referral to see a specialist. If you're lucky, the doctor will ring up the hospital and make the appointment for you. If not you'll have to call or visit the hospital yourself to make the appointment.

If you're not covered by private health insurance, you can visit the private hospitals, but you'll have to pay per consultation and per treatment which can get quite costly.

Although it comes at a price, private health care has several advantages over the state-run system, one of the main ones being that you'll get a consultation and a referral to a specialist much faster this way. Whenever I make an appointment to see the doctor at my nearest state-run centre, I usually have to wait between one and two weeks just for a consultation. With private health care, you can almost always see a doctor on the same day.

Specialist doctors in the state-run hospitals are few and far between so you can expect an even longer wait to see one of them. After one consultation at a state-run centre, I was given an appointment to see a specialist in 18 months time. I thought I had misunderstood, but when I queried it I was told that was the soonest appointment available. I cancelled my appointment and headed to the privately-run Hospiten Sur where I was seen within the hour. I had to pay around €100, but I was happy to do so to avoid the wait.

## English Doctors

If you're set on visiting an English-speaking doctor but don't want to take out private health care insurance, there is another option. You can visit one of several British doctors in Tenerife that have opened up their own practices. These doctors charge a fee of around €30-€50 for a consultation and a larger fee for treatment.

Here's a list of some of the British and English-speaking doctors currently operating in Tenerife:

- The British Surgery, Avenida Ernesto Sarti, Costa Adeje
- The British Surgery, Avenida Rafael Puig Lluvina, Las Americas
- Dr Spreafico, Edificio Simon, Los Cristianos
- Dr Karen Whittaker, next to the pharmacy inside the Arona Gran Hotel, Los Cristianos

## Registering at Your Local Health Centre

Registering at the local health centre is one aspect of relocating that many people push to one side and forget about until it's too late. Even if you've decided to opt for private health care, it's still important to register with a local doctor for one vital reason – if you need a sick note to get out of work, only state-employed doctors can hand them out, not private doctors. So although a doctor at a private health centre may treat you, you'll still need to visit a state-run doctor to prove you were too sick to work.

Once you're paying social security, you and your dependents are entitled to free health care. You'll need to travel to your nearest *Consultorio* (Doctors' Consultants) or *Centro de Salud* (Health Centre) to register.

Different centres operate during different hours – the smaller centres *(Consultorios)* are usually only open for a few hours in the morning or a few hours in the evening because there are only two doctors available. The larger centres *(Centros de Salud)* offer longer working hours because they have access to more doctors. No state-run health centres are open on the weekends.

If those working hours weren't short enough, the health centres will only accept new registrations on certain days at certain times. This means you're going to have to trek to the clinic once, just to check when you can come back to register.

When registering, you're going to have to either speak Spanish or have a Spanish-speaker with you – there won't be any interpreters and it's unlikely anyone will speak English. After telling the receptionist that you want to register, you'll need your *Certificado Registro Residente, Certificado de Empadronamiento,* social security number, passport, plus photocopies of each. If you're registering any children, you'll also need their birth certificates or *Libro de Familia* if they were born in Spain. After filling out a form or two, you and any others you're registering will be presented with medical cards which entitle you to free health care in Tenerife. Keep a hold of these cards – you'll be asked to show them when visiting the doctor and picking up a prescription.

## Before Making a Doctor's Appointment

It's worth popping into the pharmacy before you decide to make a doctor's appointment. The rules are a lot looser in Tenerife than in Britain when it comes to the kinds of medication pharmacies can hand out. You can get a hold of a lot more over-the-counter drugs without a prescription in Tenerife. The staff at most pharmacies are also quite clued-up and will be happy to suggest medicines for simple things, such as allergic reactions and general pains.

Pharmacies are generally open from 9am until 1pm and 4pm until 8pm Monday to Friday and 9am until 1pm on Saturday. There are several 24-hour pharmacies on the island which work on a rotation calendar basis.

## Making a Doctor's Appointment

Making a doctor's appointment is simple – providing you've got a grasp on the lingo. There are several ways you can do this:

- Pop into your health clinic and make an appointment at reception
- Call 012 and ask for a doctor's appointment
- Use your medical card number to log into www3.gobiernodecanarias.org/sanidad/scs/gc/ 18/Cita_Previa/index.html and make an appointment online

## In Case of Emergency

If you need medical attention urgently, head to your nearest *Urgencias* (Emergencies) section of a hospital or medical centre. Once again, it's unlikely the centre will have any interpreters and the doctors probably won't speak English. If the language barrier is going to prove to be too much of a challenge, you can head to the *Urgencias* section of the nearest private hospital where you'll have access to English-speaking doctors or interpreters. Just make sure you take your medical card and ID with you to avoid any fees.

Although you won't be charged for emergency treatment, you will be charged if you call an ambulance. The only way to get an ambulance service for free is to have a doctor call one for you.

## Dentists

Most of the dental care in Tenerife is private, with the exception of a free service for emergencies and for children. As with anywhere, fees and quality of service differ from practice to practice so it's best to ask around for recommended dentists. You can find a list of the dentists we recommend at the back of this book.

Nicola says:

"I've been using public health care since I first moved to Spain and I'm starting to get frustrated. I recently fell ill with a sinus infection – which only requires some antibiotics to clear up – and had to struggle through a fortnight in absolute agony until my doctor had time to see me. On reflection, I should have just walked into a private clinic and paid to be seen.

If you're a healthy person, I don't think private health care is worth paying for each month, but I'm all for paying for one-off appointments now and again if you want to be seen quickly."

Joe says:

"I've had private health care for over 20 years. It's expensive, about €70 per month, but the coverage is pretty good. Having said that, the only real advantage is the speed of gaining appointments and consultations, plus of course you're covered for most medical treatments and you can choose your doctor."

# 7 DAY TO DAY

## Shopping Basket

Although shops such as *Mercadona, Hiper Dino* and *Carrefour* have their own-branded lines which are cheaper than the premium brands, they're still not as cheap as their UK counterparts, mainly because of the lack of 'specials' such as 2-for-1s and weekly offers etc.

You can find a few UK items in the Spanish supermarkets, but if you're really craving some British products, you'll need to head to Iceland. There are three in Tenerife – one in Las Americas, one in Los Cristianos and one in Las Chafiras. Completely different to the Iceland chain in the UK, these shops offer a great selection of British products for those who miss a taste of home.

They're a bit more expensive than they are in the UK, but when you take into consideration shipping costs, you're still getting a good deal.

Here's a list of how much you can expect to spend on your groceries:

Loaf of English bread: €2

Loaf of Spanish bread: €1.50

One litre of UHT milk: €0.65

 12 eggs: €1.60

Box of Spanish cornflakes: €1.50

Eight litres of water: €1.50

330ml can of Coke: €0.70

500ml can of San Miguel: €0.80

Prices of fruit, vegetables, meat and fish can vary widely depending on which shop you're in and whether you're buying fresh or frozen. It's worth keeping an eye out for seasonal products and special offers if you're looking to save money. Also, try shopping for your fruit and greens at the weekly farmer's markets, such as those in Adeje or Granadilla.

Driving

Once you become familiar with driving on the right-hand side of the road and get used to giving plenty of distance to the people in rental cars who haven't got a clue where they're going, you'll find driving in Tenerife a much more pleasant experience than driving in the UK.

You can forget the hour-long traffic jams and the long commutes to work. Almost anywhere in Tenerife can be reached on road within 90 minutes. Parking can be a challenge – although there may be loads of parking spaces, you'll be pushed to find an empty one. Any parking near beaches or in the streets of main cities will fill up very fast, so you'll have to get there first thing to get a space. There are various underground car parks scattered throughout the island but they can be quite costly.

Don't even think about parking illegally because the *Grua* (pick-up truck) in Tenerife is very efficient and will take your car away before you know it. If this does happen, you'll have to go to the municipality's car pound and pay the fine to get your car back.

Although the price of it is slowly climbing, petrol is still much cheaper in Tenerife than in the UK. You'll find petrol stations lining the sides of the motorway and in several towns, offering car washing services, vacuum cleaners and air pumps, cafes and small supermarkets in addition to petrol. Bizarrely enough, most petrol stations also serve beer and other alcoholic drinks.

You'll come across many drivers that would be more at home on an F1 racing track than on the roads in Tenerife. Don't try and beat them at their own game because chances are you'll get fined for speeding. There are speed cameras located in several spots along the motorway and if you get caught, you'll have to pay a hefty fine.

Buying a Car in Tenerife

Unsurprisingly this is not as simple as in the UK.

To buy a second-hand car you'll need to pay transfer tax (*Impuesto de Transmisiones*) at the *Hacienda* (tax office), where they'll show you a contract detailing both parties details and the agreed purchase price (take your NIE and passport). Once this has been paid and stamped, take it to the *Trafico* department in Santa Cruz to change the name on the car's permit (*Permiso de Circulación*). For this, you'll need to take the following:

- Contract of purchase signed by both parties
- Copy of NIEs for both parties
- The car's Permiso de Circulación (plus a photocopy)
- The car's *Ficha Técnica*/log book (plus a photocopy)
- The car's ITV certificate (similar to MOT pass)

You can also employ the services of someone who will make the dreaded Hacienda & Trafico trip for you, such as Auto Salon (www.auto-salon.es/list.php) in Las Galletas (ask for Ferdi). It costs a bit of money (around €110 plus whatever tax is payable) but it saves you a great deal of time and faffing.

If you buy a car from a dealer, they'll sort most of the paperwork out and guide you through the process – you'll still need to take your empadronamiento and NIE number for the purchase.

Pests

There are a few kinds of creepy crawlies in Tenerife, but nothing you need to get worried about. Cockroaches are in abundance, but many complexes regularly spray the area to keep the problem down to a minimum. If your community doesn't do anything to keep the cockroaches away, you should head to your nearest *ferretería* (hardware shop) – you'll find all sorts of pest control solutions there.

Ant problems are also common – even if you keep your house squeaky clean, they take that as a challenge and will send out even larger troupes in search of food. As with cockroaches, you'll be able to find almost anything to fix your ant problem at a *ferretería*.

If you live in an area surrounded by grass and water (such as golf courses with ponds or gardens with sprinklers) you'll probably have to put up with mosquitoes. Unfortunately, there's not much you can do to keep these pests out of your home – apart from regularly dousing it with anti-mosquito spray or using plug-in-repellents.

There are some tiny jumping spiders which will give you a bite if they get the chance. If you have young children or spot a spider in your bedroom, you should get rid of it straight away. The bites aren't poisonous, but the swellings can be painful if you have an allergic reaction.

The largest pest you'll come across is the Southern Tenerife Lizard (Gallotia galloti). These lizards don't pose any kind of threat and would much rather lounge on your balcony and soak up the sun than come into your house and bother you. They'll be tempted by any food you leave on the balcony or terrace but will shoot off as soon as you chase them.

The small, pale lizards you might find clinging to your bedroom wall are geckos and according to folklore are supposed to bring good luck. They're also handy little mosquito and fly catchers so think twice about evicting the little fellas.

Business Hours

Business hours in Tenerife are very different to the ones in the UK. Banks and various government-run buildings are only open in the mornings – from around 8.30am until about 1pm from Monday to Friday.

Most shops open in the morning, close for the *siesta* and open again on an evening. The timetables are usually around 10am-1pm then 4 or 5pm-8pm Monday to Friday. Some shops will also open on a Saturday morning but won't open up again after the *siesta*. Shops in the resort centres often stay open until 9 or 10pm.

Supermarkets are generally open from 9am until 9pm Monday-Saturday with a couple also opening on Sundays, too.

Fiestas

There seem to be more and more fiestas in Tenerife every year. The island has very strong religious roots and – luckily for us – likes to celebrate its religion in the form of fiesta days when everything shuts down and almost no one works.

There are several different kinds of fiesta days – National (applies to the whole of Spain), Canarian (applies to the Canary Islands, including Tenerife) and local (applies only to the municipality). When it's a fiesta, almost all businesses and shops will be closed and public transport will be less frequent. Most bars and restaurants will stay open and the same goes for some shops in tourist areas.

The Canarians really know how to party and love their fiestas. Buzzing street parties flowing with Dorada, traditional Spanish food, live Canarian bands and salsa dancing are just some of the things you can expect.

Buses

The bus service in Tenerife is completely different to that of the UK. Instead of having a bus pass by every three minutes, it's more like every three hours.

The buses on the island are run by Titsa and are very cheap to travel on. If you're planning on using the buses often, you should buy a *Bono Bus* card. This card gives you a 30-50% discount on your bus fare and can be purchased from the bus stations and several other shops throughout the island. A *Bono Bus* card costs €15 or €25 and is valid for either one year or until you've used all the balance. It can be used by multiple people and can also be used for the tram service. The cards are a fantastic way to save money if you use public transport often and they're used by almost all the locals.

You'll find bus timetable leaflets at most of the bus stations, or you can check the times on the website. Remember to take the times with a pinch of salt – if the bus is running early, it won't hang around and if it's running late, it won't hurry up to make time. It's best to be at the stop 10 minutes beforehand just to be sure and expect to be hanging around about 30 minutes if it's late.

Website: www.titsa.com

Phone number: +34 922 531 300

<u>Language Basics</u>

Most people in the south of Tenerife will speak at least a few words of English, but it's always handy to have a grasp on the basics. There are many schools in Tenerife which offer Spanish classes and there are a handful of Spanish teachers who give lessons to groups or on a one-to-one basis.

You'll find that workers in restaurants, shops and even government offices are a lot more helpful and understanding if you make some sort of effort to speak their language – no matter how terrible you think you sound.

Keep in mind that although there is a high number of British residents, Tenerife is still a Spanish-speaking island, which means you should not expect everyone around you to speak English. If you make the effort and learn a few basic Spanish phrases, you'll find it much easier and more pleasant to get by.

To get you started, here's a list of basic Spanish vocabulary that will come in handy when you move to Tenerife:


Hello: Hola (*oh-la*)

Please: Por favor (*pour fa-vor*)

Thank you: Gracias (*grassee-ass*)

How are you?: ¿Que Tal? (*kay-tal*)

My name is…: Me llamo… (*may-yamo*)

I want: Quiero (*key-aero*)

Where is...?: ¿Dónde está...? (*don-dess-ta*)

How much?: ¿Cuánto cuesta? (*kwan-toe-kwess-ta*)

Do you speak English?: ¿Hablas Inglés? (*ablass een-glaze*)

I don't speak Spanish: No hablo Español (*no ab-low ess-pan-yol*)

# 8 CAUTIONS

## Police

Tenerife may be a small island, but law and order is provided courtesy of no less than four police forces.

The *Policia Local* (Local Police) deals with minor issues like traffic control and protection of property. They wear light blue shirts and drive in blue and white cars.

The *Policia Nacional* (National Police) deals with more serious crimes. They dress in black and drive black and white cars.

The *Policia Canaria* (Canarian Police) controls all security matters within the autonomous regions. They dress in black and drive large black and red vans.

The *Guardia Civil* (Civil Guard) is a semi-military unit which deals with drug smuggling, terrorism, bomb disposal and weapon control. They wear green uniforms and drive green and white off-road vehicles.

Remember to keep your cool and make sure you don't lose your temper or end up in an argument with any of the police officers in Tenerife for two simple reasons – they all carry guns and they're not averse to using batons to argue their point.

Driving Laws

It's still unclear as to whether you can legally drive on the roads in Tenerife with a UK licence. There are loads of British expats who haven't exchanged their UK-issued driving licence for a Spanish one and haven't come across any problems. Until the Canarian law makes it obligatory for drivers to own a Spanish licence, it's much easier to just keep hold of your UK one.

Seatbelts are compulsory and must be worn by all passengers whenever the vehicle is moving. Children under 12 are not allowed to travel in the front of the car and must sit in the back unless they're over 1.5 metres tall.

As in most countries, using a mobile phone whilst driving is illegal in Tenerife. Don't think this means you can use your phone if both hands are on the wheel and you're using headphones – driving with headphones is also illegal.

It's obligatory for all cars to carry at least one warning

triangle and two reflective jackets at all times in case of breakdown. A spare pair of glasses must also be kept in the car at all times for the driver if they wear them.

Don't expect to be able to drive home in flip flops either – if you get caught driving in any shoes without a back strap, you'll also be fined.

It's baffling why many people arrive in Tenerife (holidaymakers and residents) and think that it's ok to drink and drive abroad even though they'd never dream of doing it in the UK. If you think you can get away with it here... don't. The drink driving limit is stricter in Tenerife, with a limit of 50mg of alcohol to every 100ml of blood, which is equivalent to less than one pint of beer and just over a small (150cc) glass of wine. The police can conduct random checks and regularly set up near roundabouts late at night to catch anyone ignoring the law. If you're caught drink driving, you'll receive a huge fine or even a prison sentence.

If you receive a fine, make sure you go over the fine print. If you pay it within a certain amount of time – this will be stated on the fine – you'll receive a big discount.

Speed Restrictions

20km/h in residential areas

50km/h in built-up areas

90km/h on country roads

100km/h on dual carriageways

120km/h on motorways

Health

Residents are just as likely to fall sick as tourists so don't think you can get away with it just because you live in Tenerife.

There are no severe contagious diseases or infections in Tenerife, so as long as you have the standard adult immunizations, additional vaccinations are unnecessary.

Most of the tap water in Tenerife is undrinkable, not necessarily because it's polluted, but because it's highly-treated and will give the uninitiated a bad stomach – not to mention a nasty taste in your mouth. There are some villages located high up in the mountains that have 'purer' drinking water, but most properties will need to have a water filter installed before you're able to drink straight from the tap. You can buy bottled water from supermarkets for around €1.50 for eight litres, so make the effort and pop to the shops.

Although some resorts can be buzzing with mosquitoes at certain times of the year, Tenerife is thankfully free from malaria. If you do suffer from swarms of mosquitoes where you live, there are many options to keep them away, such as using a plug-in or roll-on repellent. If you've already been bitten by the little beasties, stop by a pharmacy and see what they can give you or take a couple of anti-histamine tablets.

The strong sun and the heat are the main causes for concern when it comes to your health. Temperatures can reach up to a sizzling 40°C+ during summer and it's even worse if the island is hit by a *calima* or *sorrocco* at the same time, both of which bring sand and dust from the Sahara, and can cause respiratory problems for asthmatics etc. You've heard it all before, but it's vital you take note of this information because in temperatures like this, it really can become a life and death situation.

During the summer months, try and stay out of direct sunlight at the hottest part of the day – between 11.30am and 2pm. If you absolutely have to be out, put plenty of suntan cream on and wear a hat and sunglasses. Sporting a strawberry-red suntan really isn't the look you want to be portraying when you're a resident (or if you're a visitor for that matter).

Dehydration is extremely common and can lead to a trip to hospital if you're not careful. Remember to drink plenty of water throughout the day (at least two litres). Alcoholic drinks dehydrate you even more, so if you're planning on spending the afternoon drinking in the sun, try and slip a few glasses of water in. It might ease the dehydration – and the hangover – the next day.

# 9 FAQS

*I have a lot of stuff I want to bring over from the UK. How can I get it to Tenerife?*

If you have more than a couple of suitcases' worth of belongings, your only option is to get your stuff shipped over or drive across Spain yourself. There are several companies offering a removal service to Tenerife, we recommend Universal Exports.

If you've decided to drive, be aware that it's going to take an absolute minimum of 4-5 days. You'll need to catch the ferry from the UK to Calais before choosing your route and driving through France and Spain. The route you pick doesn't really make a difference – as long as your final port of call in Spain is Cadiz, Seville or Huelva on the south coast. From here you can pick up the Trasmediterranea or Naviera Armas ferry directly to Santa Cruz in the north of Tenerife.

*I have a pet. Can I bring it with me?*

You can bring your furry friend with you (as long as it's not a tiger!), but you need to start looking into the necessary requirements several months before you plan on relocating. Any animal brought into the island must be micro-chipped to the ISO standard and be vaccinated against rabies. You'll also need to get a hold of an Export Health Certificate – also known as a pet's passport.

Once you've got all that sorted, you'll need to get the right size container for your pet to travel in the cargo hold. Make sure you check that the airline takes animals prior to booking your flight.

*How easy is it to get a job in Tenerife?*

In addition to having useful skills and relevant experience, your chances of finding a job in Tenerife are much better if you start networking and get to know people. With over 1/3 of Tenerife residents unemployed, jobs are few and far between, so don't expect to get the first job you apply for.

*Can I get British TV in Tenerife?*

There are two main ways you can get British TV in Tenerife – online or via a satellite. There are loads of options if you want to watch TV through the internet, just search online and you can get yourself sorted in no time. If you don't have an internet connection, you can get in touch with Premier Satellite Systems in Tenerife (www.premier-satellites.com) to set you up with a dish so you can watch your favourite British programmes.

### Are there any English-speaking banks in Tenerife?

Lloyds bank opposite the market in Costa Adeje is the most popular in Tenerife for employing the best English-speaking staff. In addition to being able to discuss everything in English, you can also get all your statements and online banking in English. If Costa Adeje is too far out of the way for you, don't worry – many banks in Tenerife now employ English-speaking staff, just make sure you check before you sign up.

### Is it really sunny all-year-round?

The short answer is: yes – it really is sunny all-year-round... almost. Between November and February Tenerife usually experiences a couple of storms with strong winds and buckets of rain for a few days, but that's it. The rest of the year it's pretty much warm and sunny.

### Is it safe living on a volcanic island?

Nobody can give any guarantees but the chances of a catastrophic volcanic eruption are slim to say the least. I doubt anybody on the island loses sleep over the fear of Teide erupting.

# 10 USEFUL INFO

Electricity in Tenerife is set at 220 volts which means all UK appliances will work without a problem but anything from the US will require a voltage converter. To use any appliances brought over from another country, you'll need an adapter which can be bought from most Tenerife supermarkets for a lot cheaper than back in the UK.

Unlike Spain, Tenerife runs on GMT – the same time as the UK. This means you don't have to change any clocks and won't accidentally call someone back home at 3am.

Residents in the Canary Islands enjoy a special resident discount on many things. As long as you have the correct documentation (see chapter 'Becoming Legal') you can get a 50% discount on all flights within Spain and other discounts on various attractions and activities within the Canary Islands.

For savings on bars, restaurants and other services, it's worth investing a small amount in a Green Banana discount card and/or mobile app (www.greenbananaguide.com).

## Emergencies

- All: 112
- National police: 091
- Local police: 092
- Ambulance: 061
- Fire brigade: 080
- Guardia Civil: 062

## English-Speaking Doctors

- The British Surgery, Avenida España, Costa Adeje
- The British Surgery, Avenida Ernesto Sarti, Costa Adeje
- Perfect Health, CC Fañabe Plaza, Costa Adeje
- The British Surgery, Avenida Rafael Puig Lluvina, Las Americas
- Dr Spreafico, Edificio Simon, Los Cristianos
- Dr Karen Whittaker, next to the pharmacy inside the Arona Gran Hotel, Los Cristianos

## Hospitals in the south

- Costa Adeje, San Eugenio – 922 752 626
- Hospiten Sur, Las Americas – 922 750 022

# ABOUT THE AUTHORS

## Nicola Quinn

Nicola didn't move to Tenerife in search of a change in lifestyle, in fact she didn't decide to move to the island at all – she was shipped along with the rest of her parents' belongings back in 2002.

She went to a British school in Tenerife where her interest in writing first began. Thankfully, the school drummed Spanish lessons into the pupils' heads daily so she's now fluent which makes getting all the dull yet important things done in Tenerife so much easier.

Since she had spent a lot of her childhood in Tenerife and felt like it was her real home, Nicola decided against returning to the UK to pursue her studies like her friends. Instead she focused on getting work on the island and being able to support herself whilst also enjoying the fantastic weather and laid-back culture that the UK just couldn't compete with.

In addition to writing, Nicola's other passion is cooking. When she's not scribbling in a notebook or tapping the keys of a keyboard she can be found in the kitchen trying out a new recipe or wandering around a farmers' market searching for fresh ingredients. In 2011, Nicola found a way to bring her two greatest passions together and began her own food blog (www.pinkrecipebox.com) where she keeps track of all her recipes and foodie travels.

Nicola works as a social media manager and dabbles in freelance travel writing. Most of her working week is spent cooped up inside an office, so come Friday afternoon she's ready to burst into the great outdoors and make the most of her weekend.

## Joe Cawley

Joe Cawley is a freelance travel writer and author based in Tenerife. His work has been published in a range of publications from *The Sunday Times*, *Express* and *Guardian* to *The New York Post*, *Taipei Times* and *Conde Naste Traveler* amongst others. He's the author of Kindle bestseller, *More Ketchup than Salsa: Confessions of a Tenerife Barman* which was voted 'Best Travel Narrative' by the British Guild of Travel Writers, and has contributed to several guidebooks including titles by Dorling Kindersley and Lonely Planet.

For two years, Joe was the managing editor of Living Tenerife magazine, the first high quality glossy to grace the archipelago's shores. Following a deskbound stint, he returned to the world of far-flung freelance commissions.

His specialities have evolved relative to his own biological clock; from hedonistic holidays for hormone ravaged teenagers, budget jaunts for the financially-bereft, travelling with tearaway toddlers, to spa breaks for the tired and needy. All have become niches well-versed in Joe's repertoire.

Soft adventure forays include getting lost in the Peruvian Amazon; paddling upstream in the jungles of Nicaragua with a Sandinista; husky-sledding in Lapland; and wolf- and bear-tracking in Romania.

Joe currently lives in the hills of Guia de Isora with his family and an assortment of other wildlife. As well as writing, Joe also runs Tenerife's number one online travel guide, My Destination Tenerife (www.mydestination.com/Tenerife).

You can follow Joe on his blog (www.joecawley.co.uk)

Gracias, and indeed thanks, for buying this guide on Moving to Tenerife. If you have any comments or questions, we'd be glad to hear from you, although remember we're not legal experts so won't be able to help along those lines.

We both wish you luck in your move to Tenerife. It really is a fantastic place to live and if you do follow your dreams, we hope it proves to be the best decision you ever made.

Joe & Nicola

X

PS If you've enjoyed reading this guide and have found it useful, it would help immensely if you would take a few minutes to leave a comment/review on Amazon.

Thanks.

OTHER BOOKS BY THE AUTHORS:

*More Ketchup than Salsa* by Joe Cawley

ISBN: 095724990X

"Brilliant book... very funny..."

"Fantastic, hilarious, painful. Probably the best book I have read this millenium!"

When Joe and Joy decide to trade in their life on a cold fish market to run a bar in the sub-tropical sunshine, they anticipate a paradise of sea, sand and siestas. Little did they expect their foreign fantasy to turn out to be about as exotic as a wet Monday morning.

A hilarious insight into the wild and wacky characters of an expat community in a holiday destination, More Ketchup than Salsa is a must-read for anybody who has ever dreamed about jetting off to sunnier climes, finding a job abroad... or anybody who has even momentarily flirted with the idea of 'doing a Shirley Valentine' in these trying economic times.